REJECTION AND EMOTIONAL ABUSE

by Jonas Clark

Unless otherwise noted, Scripture quotations are taken from the King James Version.

HEALING REJECTION & EMOTIONAL ABUSE

ISBN-10: 1-886885-37-0
ISBN-13: 978-1-886885-37-0

Published by Spirit of Life Publishing
27 West Hallandale Beach Blvd.
Hallandale, Florida, 33009-5437, U.S.A.
(954) 456-4420

www.JonasClark.com

HEALING REJECTION & EMOTIONAL ABUSE

Everyone comes face-to-face with rejection. It is a part of everyday life. We can't avoid rejection because we can't control the way people feel about us. Some will like us automatically; others may reject us without reason. The good news is, however, we can control our response

R ejection wants to give you a skewed identity. It is a force that will try to mold your personality into something pitiful. If you are suffering from rejection, remember this: the rejected personality is not the real you. The real you is hidden under the mask of rejection. The good news is you can take off that mask and live the life God has purposed for you. There is life after rejection. It's a life of love, acceptance, joy and peace.

We can't let our hurts of yesterday decide our identity today. You are who God says you are. Renewing your mind with the Word of God is the first step toward freedom from rejection. If we do not think right, then we cannot believe right. If we do not believe right, then we will never be able to act right.

It is important to understand that we cannot trust our soulish nature to tell us who we are. The house that rejection built is supplied with inner agony and an endless struggle to feel accepted. Past experiences, however, will always taint and falsely color the way we see ourselves and the way we respond to those around us. In other words, even when we are accepted we may not feel accepted.

RENOVATING THE OLD HOUSE

Again, our rejected experiences have built a house according to the designs of pain and hurt. If we want to get free from the past we will eventually have to undertake one of two projects, depending on how much damage has been done. Sometimes we need to renovate our minds with the truth of God's Word. But, like any renovation, sometimes the damage is so deep or so old that renovation turns into complete reconstruction. In those cases, the old house must be torn down to its foundation and built again.

Remember, freedom from rejection depends, in part, on the success of your renovation project. So what does renew mean and how do we undertake this renovation project? Let's look to God's Word for answers.

> "And be not conformed to this world: but be ye transformed by the renewing (renovation) of your mind, that ye may prove what is that good, and acceptable, and perfect, will of God" (Romans 12:2).

The English Word transformed stems from the Greek Word *metamorphoo*, meaning to be changed into another form. This suggests the Word of God, when used to renovate our minds, will gradually morph us into the proper personality. It promises life after rejection by the washing of the water of the Word.

Notice Romans 12:2 deals with the mind of man and not the spirit of man. When you repented of your sins and asked Jesus for forgiveness, you became a new creature in Christ Jesus,

> "Old things are passed away; behold, all things are become new" (2 Corinthians 5:17).

That dealt with your spirit man, however, the real you. But your soul man still had issues that needed to be dealt with.

The soul of man is the mind, will, intellect, reasoning, imaginations and emotions. All of these must be conformed to the will of God through submission to the Word of God. Only then can our personalities be morphed into our proper, Christ-like identities.

Don't look at the Word of God's ability to renovate our minds through the eyes of unbelief. Meditating on God's Word will bring freedom from even the deepest pain if we only believe. But if we reject the knowledge of God, the pain of rejection will continue to tell us who we are. Rejection is a liar. God's word is truth. Applied knowledge of the Word of God is key to the success of our renovation project. We don't need to understand how or why it works. We need only have faith and be doers of the word to find life after rejection. Remember the words the Lord spoke through the Prophet Hosea:

> "My people are destroyed for lack of knowledge: because thou hast rejected knowledge, I will also reject thee...." (Hosea 4:6)

REJECTING KNOWLEDGE

Rejection of knowledge (God's Word) gives rejection the right to continue to operate. The Word teaches us that if we are "hearers only" and not "doers of the Word" of God, then we "deceive ourselves." Doubtless, if we deceive ourselves we will continue to walk in the rejected personality. The applied Word of God is our key to victory!

> "But be ye doers of the Word, and not hearers only, deceiving your own selves. For if any be a hearer of the Word, and not a doer, he is like unto a man beholding his natural face in a glass: For he beholdeth himself, and goeth his way, and straightway forgetteth what manner (sort) of man he was. But whoso

looketh into the perfect law of liberty, and continueth therein, he being not a forgetful hearer, but a doer of the work, this man shall be blessed in his deed." (James 1:22-25)

The English word in the Bible that reads deceive stems from the Greek Word *paralogizomai*, meaning to:

- Reckon wrongly.

- Cheat yourself.

- Have a false reasoning.

- Delude.

- Avoid.

The bottom line is this:

Deception is a condition that is caused by refusing to walk out (obey) the Word of God.

Yes, there may have and probably was an event that sent rejection knocking at your door. But you have to let it into your house. This is tough love, but I have to be honest with you. It is impossible to renovate your mind with truth if you do not obey the truth. Renovation is a process of tearing down the learned behavior that rejection built. The truth we obey is the truth that will tear down the rejected personality.

CAUSES OF REJECTION

Everyone comes face-to-face with rejection. It is a part of everyday life. We can't avoid rejection because we can't control the way people feel about us. Some will like us automatically; others may reject us without reason. The good news is, however, we can control our response.

What does rejection in everyday life look like? Well, people might be turned down for pay raises, refused job promotions, declined for loans, taken for granted by peers, treated poorly by family, and passed over for due recognition. All of these are real life situations in which people are rejected. It may not seem as dramatic as a divorce or an abuse, but it's rejection all the same. So why do some face more difficulty handling every day rejections than others? Could it have more to do with the feelings that are set off inside their souls even at the slightest hint of rejection? Consider this: Is rejection an emotional response or an objective response to life? Does rejection push a button causing some sort of internal process that calculates a lessened self-worth? As we continue along in our study, let's explore the possibility the negative feelings rejection causes are rooted in the improper internalization of external events.

Each of us has the basic need to feel accepted. Rejection is the feeling (internalization) that we are not being valued or accepted. When we do not feel accepted, then we must learn how to deal with the negative feelings of that rejection because we cannot depend on being accepted by others to give us our sense of self-worth. Jesus Christ makes us worthy, and we are "accepted in the beloved" (Ephesians 1:6).

Before we can properly respond to rejection events, we must pinpoint the source of the feelings. This is what I call rejection's trigger. Rejection's trigger must be dismantled. Interestingly, there are almost as many causes for rejection as there are people. Causes of rejection can stem from:

- A lack of love from a spouse, parent, or grandparent.
- An unwanted pregnancy.
- The trauma of divorce.
- The abandonment by a friend or loved one.
- A violation of trust.
- Abuse, whether physical, emotional, or sexual.
- Public humiliation.
- A failure.
- A bankruptcy.
- Poor performance academically or in sports.

DISCOVERY CHECKLIST

Do you respond out of a rejection-based personality? The list of questions below is designed to help you uncover rejection-based responses and lifestyles. Take your time as you prayerfully read the list, and let the Holy Spirit speak to your heart. Now is the time to be honest with yourself. You are reading this book because you are trying to understand rejection and find God's path to emotional healing. Answering these questions truthfully will help you learn more about yourself and help you more effectively minister to others. As you read the questions, put a check mark beside those things that trouble you.

☐ Do you have a fear of people's opinion of you?

☐ Are you a perfectionist?

☐ Are you frustrated with life?

☐ Are you abnormally anxious?

☐ Do you project a false sense of superiority?

☐ Are you suspicious of anything nice done for you?

☐ Do you have difficulty trusting God and others?

☐ Do you have difficulty understanding the love of God?

☐ Do you have difficulty showing love to others?

☐ Do you think that God cannot use you?

☐ Do you ask yourself, "How can God love me?"

☐ To "feel special" will you do extreme things like dangerous sports?

☐ Do you have severe bouts with depression and thoughts of suicide?

☐ Do you hide behind pets, books, hobbies, or work?

☐ Do you overemphasize material possessions? What about in dress or appearance?

☐ Do you have a dominating air or way about you?

☐ Do you have a critical spirit?

☐ Have you entered a self-imposed isolation from others?

☐ Do you feel empty and unfulfilled?

☐ Do you have a difficult time receiving love?

☐ Are there times when you don't want anyone to touch you?

☐ Do you value acceptance and hate correction?

☐ Do you have feelings of inferiority?

☐ Do you think that God does not love you as much as others?

☐ Do you dress to get attention?

☐ Do you have a fear of communicating your opinions?

☐ Do you detest being compared to others?

☐ Do you have uncontrolled bouts with pent up anger?

☐ Are there times when you feel undeserving?

☐ Do you feel that your lot in life is to suffer?

☐ Do you have a fear of failure?

☐ Are you a workaholic or overachiever?

☐ Do you take things too personally?

☐ Would you rather spend time with your pets or animals than people?

☐ Do you have a woe-is-me, gloomy view of life?

☐ Are you afraid to tell the truth about your feelings?

☐ Do you constantly fight discouragement?

☐ Are you harshly judgmental of others?

☐ Are you a faultfinder?

☐ Are you afraid of God?

☐ Are you always on the defensive?

☐ Do you have a problem relating to the opposite sex?

☐ Are you a procrastinator?

☐ Do you feel stupid, inferior, or self-conscious when around other people?

☐ Do you resent and hold bitterness toward others?

☐ Do you feel like you need to seek attention from others?

☐ Do you feel like you can never measure up to others?

☐ Are you driven to prove yourself to others?

☐ Are you troubled with constant mind traffic that gives you no rest?

☐ Do you have a problem saying, 'No' when you know that you need to?

☐ Do you feel threatened by others?

☐ Do you attack those you love and don't understand why?

☐ Do you think that no one understands you?

☐ Are you drawn towards base people who seem to be more accepting of you, yet do nothing to bring stability in your life?

☐ Are you sometimes introverted and at other times extroverted?

☐ Do you avoid being involved in group activities?

☐ Do you try to fit in with the crowd but never feel that you belong?

The checklist above is provided only to stir your thinking and allow the Holy Spirit reveal some of the root causes of why you feel the way you do. Once we recognize rejection, then we can begin the healing and rebuilding process. If you checked several of the items on the list, perhaps you are having difficulty with rejection. Don't worry – I have great news for you. Jesus is the answer to all your problems. He understands you better than you understand yourself. He has offered us a way of escape. His Word will teach you what to do. There is hope for you! There is life after rejection.

ISBN 1-886885-04-4

WANT MORE?
Read Jezebel, Seducing Goddess of War

The Jezebel spirit wants to control your life – and then she wants to destroy it. Jezebel is a warring, contending spirit that uses flattery and manipulation to create soul ties that she uses to control her victims… and she's targeting you. Find out how to recognize this spirit's wicked operations, which include false prophecy, fear tactics, seduction and many other wiles. This book will expose this controlling spirit for what it is with explicit details, intriguing personal testimonies and letters from believers who have battled this foe. Don't tolerate Jezebel… get equipped and gain victory over this spirit today!

Revelation about Jezebel is one thing – practical ways to overcome her is another. Find out how to deal with this wicked spirit today!

To order, log on to www.JonasClark.com or call 800.943.6490.

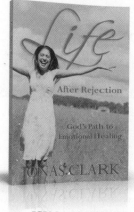

ISBN 1-886885-22-2

Life After Rejection: God's Path to Emotional Healing

Rejection comes from hurts and wounds. It holds you hostage to wrong feelings, behaviors and attitudes. If you've been betrayed, divorced, abandoned or abused, or even if you were simply turned down for a job or shunned by a social group, you have been affected by rejection.

This book was written for you. Find how to...

- Identify the roots of rejection and get rid of them.
- Break free from feelings of worthlessness and guilt.
- Receive God's love, acceptance and emotional healing.
- Find fast freedom from depression attacks.
- Help others find victory too!
- And much more...

To order, log on to www.JonasClark.com or call 800.943.6490.

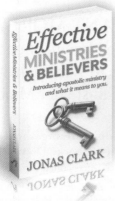

ISBN 1-886885-25-7

EFFECTIVE MINISTRIES & BELIEVERS:
INTRODUCING APOSTOLIC MINISTRY AND WHAT IT MEANS TO YOU

Christ's disciples have fought raging spiritual battles with Satan for centuries. Some failed, others experienced limited success, but there is another group of effective believers that discovered the secret to victorious living. This group was taught by apostles that Christ would "build His Church and the gates of hell would not prevail against it."

Those who want to do great exploits for Christ need to read this book.

Discover your authority:
- How the apostles taught believers to turn the world upside down.
- How apostolic design empowers every believer for breakthrough.
- How to become a spiritual warrior, reformer and prophetic strategist.
- How apostolic restoration and reformation principles advance your calling.

To order, log on to www.JonasClark.com or call 800.943.6490.

PROPHECY WITHOUT PERMISSION

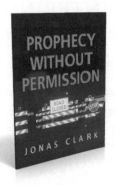

ISBN 1-886885-31-1

Presumptous prophets prophesy because they can, but should they? Does a prophet need permission to prophesy? If a prophet who has not been granted permission to prophesy and yet does, is he guilty of sin.

Prophetic ministry is important and so is accuracy.
Learn these truths:

- How prophets stay accurate.
- Why prophecy by faith alone is dangerous.
- How to avoid the spirit of divination.
- Five steps to prophetic release.
- Prophetic Mantels and Activation.
- Receiving prophetic permission.

To order, log on to www.JonasClark.com or call 800.943.6490.

ENTERING PROPHETIC MINISTRY

Prophets carry a great sense of spiritual authority. They enjoy rooting out pulling down and destroying all spiritual opposition that gets in the way of the plans and purpose of God.

In this book discover:

- How prophets see what others cannot.
- Why prophets carry a great sense of spiritual authority.
- Why prophets are the most spiritually sensitive of all the five-fold ministry gifts.
- How prophets steward the mysteries of God.
- How prophets challenge dead traditions of men and dangerous spirits of religion.
- How to enter prophetic ministry.
- Receiving prophetic permission.

Equipping Resources by Jonas Clark

Pocket-Size Books

What To Do When You Feel Like Giving Up

Healing Rejection & Emotional Abuse

Entering Prophetic Ministry

The Weapons of Your Warfare

Prophecy Without Permission

Overcoming Dark Imaginations

How Witchcraft Spirits Attack

Unlocking Prophetic Imaginations

Seeing What Others Can't

Books

Extreme Prophetic Studies

Advanced Apostolic Studies

Kingdom Living: How to Activate Your Spiritual Authority

Imaginations: Dare to Win the Battle Against Your Mind

Jezebel, Seducing Goddess of War *(Also Available in Spanish)*

Exposing Spiritual Witchraft

30 Pieces of Silver *(Overcoming Religious Spirits)*

The Apostolic Equipping Dimension

Effective Ministries & Believers

Life After Rejection: God's Path to Emotional Healing

Come Out! A Handbook for the Serious Deliverance Minister

www.JonasClark.com